THE TRUTH ABOUT SALVATION

april a. tapanes

THE TRUTH ABOUT
SALVATION

TATE PUBLISHING & *Enterprises*

Tate Publishing
& Enterprises

Tate Publishing is committed to excellence in the publishing industry. Our staff of highly trained professionals, including editors, graphic designers, and marketing personnel, work together to produce the very finest books available. The company reflects the philosophy established by the founders, based on Psalms 68:11,

"THE LORD GAVE THE WORD AND GREAT WAS THE COMPANY OF THOSE WHO PUBLISHED IT."

If you would like further information, please contact us:
1.888.361.9473 | www.tatepublishing.com
TATE PUBLISHING & *Enterprises*, LLC | 127 E. Trade Center Terrace
Mustang, Oklahoma 73064 USA

Published in the United States of America

ISBN: 978-1-5988697-8-1

07.05.22

I would like to dedicate this study to my precious and almighty God who is faithful and proved by having this study published that He can use anyone—even a nobody like me.

> Here is a trustworthy saying that deserves full acceptance: Christ Jesus came into the world to save sinners—of whom I am the worst. But for that very reason I was shown mercy so that in me, the worst of sinners, Christ Jesus might display his unlimited patience as an example for those who would believe on him and receive eternal life. Now to the King eternal, immortal, invisible, the only God, be honor and glory for ever and ever. Amen.
>
> 1 Timothy 1: 15–17

Introduction

I am so glad that you have chosen this study! You are about to experience a four week adventure that is designed to help you dive in to God's Word and establish a time with Him each day. You will see first hand how awesome God really is and how He desires an intimate relationship with you. You will be amazed at how God will work in your life if you are faithful and spend time with Him each day.

Before you begin, make sure you have the following supplies to get you started: pencil and/or pen, highlighter, your Bible (use whatever translation you prefer–most of the references in this study are from the NIV), and a journal (optional). I know that some people do not like to journal, however, it can be a wonderful tool. By using a journal, you can keep a record of what God is saying to you as well as write any scripture that you want to remember. I find that when I write scripture, it is easier for me to remember. If you have a desire to get more from the study, I would strongly suggest that you keep a journal.

Each of the four weeks is broken down into five days each and takes approximately 15 to 20 minutes per day. It is most important to pray before you begin a day. Ask God to show you what He wants you to learn and to show you how you can apply what He shows you to your life. Once you have prayed, read the scripture referenced at the beginning of the day. Make sure to answer all the questions even if they seem too simple or too hard–the questions are there to get you thinking so make sure and answer them. If you are struggling with a question, reread the referenced scripture and continue to reread it until you come up with an answer. Don't worry–I will explain each question for the day so you can see what point I was trying to make. Just stick with it and you will see God doing an amazing work in your life.

Now the adventure begins! Have a wonderful time in God's Word and God bless you.

WEEK 1

What is Salvation?

This is a commonly asked question by many people from many different backgrounds. The simplest way to define salvation: spending eternity in heaven with God. In today's society there are many different opinions on how salvation is achieved and opinions are treated as truth. Opinions are *only* opinions and not truth! There can only be one truth and the truth is only found in God's Word, the Bible. This week we will look at what God's Word says about salvation and review sound doctrine concerning salvation.

DAY 1

Who Needs Salvation?

Begin today's lesson by reading Romans 3:9–18.

Who is under sin? _Every one_

Who is righteous? _No one_

In most translations of the Bible, the phrase "no one" or "none" is repeated 4 times between verses 10 and 12. Wow! When God's Word repeats itself, it should be taken very seriously. It is very clear that *all* people are under sin. It does not matter what your status is in society, who you know, how good you have been, or how many good deeds you've done—because of Adam and Eve's sin, you and I were born under sin.

> The fool says in his heart, "There is no God." They are corrupt, their deeds are vile; there is no one who does good. The LORD looks down from heaven on the sons of men to see if there are any who understand, any who seek God. All have turned aside, they have together become corrupt; there is no one who does good, not even one.
>
> Psalm 14:1–3, NIV

What is God looking for?

righteous people

Everyone is in need of salvation. Everyone needs the Savior. God looks down from heaven searching for anyone who really longs to know Him and He finds no one. Why is that? *"For out of the heart come evil thoughts, murder, adultery, sexual immorality, theft, false testimony, slander."* (Matthew 15:19, NIV). God is holy and cannot be in the presence of sin, therefore, he cannot allow anyone with sin in their heart to enter heaven. He had to provide a plan to cleanse us of our sin so that we could be in his presence. The fact is that no one is good enough for God on their own because people do not naturally seek after God–they love sin. People satisfy their love of sin by satisfying their flesh and not their spirit. The flesh is the five senses: sight, touch, taste, feel, and hearing. The sin nature is satisfied when one or more of the senses receive pleasure; whereas, the spirit can only receive pleasure from the spirit. Jesus said it perfectly in John 3:5–7:

> "I tell you the truth, no one can enter the kingdom
> of God unless he is born of water and the Spirit.
> Flesh gives birth to flesh, but the Spirit] gives birth to

spirit. You should not be surprised at my saying, 'You must be born again.' "

Whoever believes in him is not condemned, but whoever does not believe stands condemned already because he has not believed in the name of God's one and only Son. This is the verdict: Light has come into the world, but men loved darkness instead of light because their deeds were evil. Everyone who does evil hates the light, and will not come into the light for fear that his deeds will be exposed.

John 3:18–20, NIV

Society constantly tells us to follow our hearts because our hearts are right. That's the problem—society and God's Word do not agree! In fact they are exact opposites! God is clear in Jeremiah 17:9, *"The heart is deceitful above all things and beyond cure. Who can understand it?"* At this point you have to decide whom to believe: your friends, the television, or any other worldly information or God who created you. Unfortunately, most people choose the world because that is what their heart tells them to do and they miss out on God and his wonderful gift of salvation. Let me make one thing clear, when faced with whom to believe, God or society, choose God! Only God is true and just and He will *never* mislead you. Only God can be trusted–not your heart. A person can follow their heart right to hell.

Society also says that all religions are equal and are different ways to achieve the same goal of going to heaven. In other words, if you are a good Muslim, a good Buddhist, a good Jehovah's Witness, you have eternal life or have achieved salvation. Let's see what God's Word says.

> Enter through the narrow gate. For wide is the gate and broad is the road that leads to destruction, and many enter through it. But small is the gate and narrow the road that leads to life, and only a few find it.
>
> Matthew 7:13–14, NIV

> Therefore Jesus said again, "I tell you the truth, I am the gate for the sheep. All who ever came before me were thieves and robbers, but the sheep did not listen to them. I am the gate; whoever enters through me will be saved. He will come in and go out, and find pasture."
>
> John 10:7–9, NIV

What is the narrow gate?

Salvation

Who is the gate?

Jesus _____

The narrow gate is salvation and the gate is Jesus. Salvation is only possible through Jesus. The Bible clearly tells us that there is no other way to receive salvation. *"Jesus answered, 'I am the way and the truth and the life. No one comes to the Father except through me.'"* (John 14:6, NIV). If there was another way, Jesus died on the cross for nothing! As a matter of fact, the name Jesus means salvation. Any religion that denies that Jesus is God in the flesh is a false religion; therefore, there is no salvation. Think of how ridiculous it is to say all religions are equal. If that were so, there would be no reason for Jesus's death on the cross or a need for salvation.

> "Who is the liar? It is the man who denies that Jesus is the Christ. Such a man is the antichrist—he denies the Father and the Son. No one who denies the Son has the Father; whoever acknowledges the Son has the Father also."
>
> 1 John 2:22–23, NIV

The word Christ means anointed one or Messiah. In other words, 1 John 2:22 reads as, *"Who is the liar? It is the man who denies that Jesus is the messiah.1"* Also the word antichrist simply means against Christ. God's Word is clear; anyone who denies that Jesus is the messiah is actually an enemy of God. Are you an enemy of God?

God created each and every one of us. He loves everybody and wants everyone to spend eternity with Him in heaven. That's why He made salvation available to all people no matter where they were born, what nationality they are, or what color skin they have. God doesn't look at anything but the heart! All he wants is for us to trust him and depend on him. We have a tendency to want to take control of our lives and situations. God wants us to trust Him enough to relinquish our hold on the reigns of life and let him work through us to grow us into the people He created us to be. Our God is an awesome God who can do anything and does! He alone has the power to change hearts, turn lost lives around, and bring us into harmony and fellowship with Him. When King David had an affair with Bathsheba and had her husband Uriah murdered in battle, God used Nathan the prophet to point out David's sin and God changed his heart. When Saul who later became Paul hated Christians and had them imprisoned, Jesus met him on the road and turned his life around. Paul went from trying to destroy the church to building the church. If God can work in the lives of King David and Paul, He can certainly work in your life!

What has God said to you today?

_____

_____

_____

_____

_____

_____

DAY 2

Was Jesus' Death Necessary?

As we saw in day one, the gate or way to God is Jesus. Was Jesus's death really necessary? Since Jesus is the only way to God, couldn't God find another way to deliver us from our sin? As we will see, the only way for salvation is through the shed blood of Jesus Christ. Let's see what God's Word says. Read Leviticus 16.

What animals were to be sacrificed by Aaron?

Bull, ram; goats

Who was Aaron making atonement for?

he + family, + people

What did Aaron do with the bull's blood?

Sprinkle in front of atonement cover (held 10 comm.)

What did Aaron do with the goat's blood?

Same

What was the purpose of the animal's blood?

make atonement for sins of Israelites

Aaron had to sacrifice a bull and a goat. The bull was for his family and the goat was for Israel. It was very important that Aaron's relationship be right with God before he made the sacrifice or he would die just like his sons did when they approached the Lord. That is why Aaron had to sacrifice the bull first for himself and his family. Aaron, the high priest, had to atone for his and his family sins before he could make atonement for the sins of Israel. His relationship had to be reconciled before he could reconcile Israel's relationship to God. Jesus is our high priest and when he died on the cross he took on all our sin. That caused Jesus to be separated from God as we are separated from God because God cannot be in the presence of sin—He is a holy God. That is why Jesus cried, *"My God, my God, why have you forsaken me?"* in Matthew 27:46 (NIV). Through his own perfect blood, he was able to reconcile himself to God the Father before he reconciled us. Jesus restored his relationship before restoring ours. This is shown so clearly in the Day of Atonement and how the high priest reconciled his family and the nation through the shed blood. The Day of Atonement was the only day sins could be forgiven and the only day the high priest could enter the Holy of Holies. Jesus is our high priest that has full access to the Holy of Holies everyday and the only way to be forgiven is through His shed blood for us.

> "In fact, the law requires that nearly everything be cleansed with blood, and without the shedding of blood there is no forgiveness."

> Hebrews 9:22, NIV

Notice that both the bull's blood and the goat's blood had to put on the atonement cover and sprinkled in front of it seven times in order to be reconciled before God. This is a beautiful picture because the atonement cover was the lid to the Ark of the Covenant which held the Ten Commandments. This is a foreshadowing of Christ because the blood of Christ would cover the law and only through his blood can we have access to God.

"In him we have redemption through his blood, the forgiveness of sins, in accordance with the riches of God's grace that he lavished on us with all wisdom and understanding."

Ephesians 1:7–8, NIV

With out the death of Christ, there would be no salvation! In order for anyone to have eternal life, Christ had to defeat death through his resurrection!

"Therefore, just as sin entered the world through one man, and death through sin, and in this way death came to all men, because all sinned . . . Consequently, just as the result of one trespass was condemnation for all men, so also the result of one act of righteousness was justification that brings life for all men."

Romans 5:12, 18, NIV

There is no other way to receive salvation than through the blood of Christ. Since Adam brought sin into the world, Jesus had to redeem us. Just like the animal sacrifice had to be a perfect animal with no defects, Jesus had no sin. Only a perfect man could redeem us because sin cannot stand before a holy God. Jesus is fully God and fully man!

"But if we walk in the light, as he is in the light, we have fellowship with one another, and the blood of Jesus, his Son, purifies us from all sin."

1 John 1:7, NIV

What has God said to you today?

_____

_____

_____

_____

_____

_____

Take a moment and thank God for his wonderful son who paid for your sin—a debt that no one else could have paid.

DAY 3

A Free Gift

God is so good and he gives wonderful gifts to us; however, there is one gift that he gives freely to whoever wants it. It's there for the taking–all that we have to do is receive it. What could this gift possibly be? Let's begin to see what this gift is by reading John 4:1–26.

What town did Jesus go through on his way to Galilee?

_____

Why is this important?

_____

What is the "gift of God" in verse 10?

_____

What is the water that Jesus is referring to in verse 14?

_____

_____

_____

How is God to be worshiped?

_____

_____

Who did Jesus identify himself as to the Samaritan woman?

_____

On Jesus's way to Galilee, he went through Samaria where he met a woman at a well. The woman was surprised that Jesus even spoke to her because he was a Jew. The Jews did not like the Samaritans at all because they were not "real" Jews. The Samaritans were a mixed race of Assyrians and Jews who practiced a form of the Jewish religion. This did not matter to Jesus because he saw the woman's heart and knew she needed the Savior. Jesus met her where she was at–He went out of his way to meet her. That shows how important our relationship is to God. God comes to us!

> "The Spirit and the bride say, "Come!" And let him who hears say, "Come!" Whoever is thirsty, let him come; and whoever wishes, let him take the free gift of the water of life."
>
> Revelation 22:17, NIV

God's gift to us is the Holy Spirit and this precious gift cannot be earned. That means we can only receive the gift through God's grace.

> "Peter replied, 'Repent and be baptized, every one of you, in the name of Jesus Christ for the forgiveness of your sins. And you will receive the gift of the Holy Spirit.'"

> Acts 2:38, NIV

> "Whoever believes in me, as the Scripture has said, streams of living water will flow from within him." By this he meant the Spirit, whom those who believed in him were later to receive. Up to that time the Spirit had not been given, since Jesus had not yet been glorified.

> John7:38–39, NIV

The water that Jesus talks about is the Holy Spirit because it is our spiritual life. Just like the human body cannot survive without water, the soul cannot have eternal life without the Holy Spirit. The only way to receive the Holy Spirit is by believing Jesus Christ is God, and that he died for your sins, and ask him into your heart. Until that happens, there is no way the "living water" can live in you.

The only way to worship God is in spirit and in truth. What does that mean? What spirit? First you have to understand what worship means. Worship is not something that we only do on Sundays; it is how we express our love and gratitude to the almighty creator! That is supposed to be done everyday. The only spirit that can know how to worship God is His spirit, the Holy Spirit. Since the Holy Spirit is God, he knows how to teach us God's Word and how to show God our love.

> Until the Holy Spirit lives in you, you have no spirit. When God created us, he made us a triune creation: body, soul, spirit. The body is our flesh and bones. The soul is everything that makes us who we are: personality, emotions, behavior, etc. The spirit is for worshiping God. When Adam sinned and ate the forbidden fruit, the spirit immediately died, the soul became corrupted, and the body began to decay. When the spirit died, the relationship between God and man was severed and the Savior was needed. 2

When the human spirit died, it left a hole in our being! The only way to fill that hole is to accept God's precious gift of the Holy Spirit. Without the Holy Spirit, there is no satisfaction, only distraction! People try to replace God with money, status, hobbies, friends, relationships—whatever. The truth is that there will be no peace or fulfillment until the Holy Spirit lives in you!

For the wages of sin is death, but the gift of God is eternal life in Christ Jesus our LORD.

Romans 6:23, NIV

You can be confident that God's Word is eternal truth! It is popular in today's society to not have absolutes. Everything is based on situational morality that is established by the individual. The problem is that different people have different morals for whatever reasons. When God is removed, there is no truth. God is an absolute so to believe in God is to have absolutes!

Jesus identified himself as the Messiah. There are many times in scripture that Jesus does this. I know that several other religions see Jesus as a prophet but Jesus was not a prophet! Jesus was and is the living God! His whole purpose for living was to die a horrible death on the cross so you could go to heaven. Had Jesus not died on the cross, there would be no hope for anyone because there would be no salvation.

Thanks be to God for his indescribable gift!

2 Corinthians 9:15, NIV

Take the time today to sing or pray the chorus of this old Hymn.

Thank you, Lord, *for saving my soul,*
Thank you, Lord, *for making me whole;*
Thank you, Lord, *for giving to me*
Thy great salvation so rich and free.

DAY 4

Eternal Guarantee

What is a guarantee? A guarantee is a promise or assurance of something that can be in writing. Do you know that God has given you a guarantee in writing? This guarantee is your salvation! That's right, there is nothing you can do to lose your salvation. Let's see what God's Word says about this.

> Now it is God who has made us for this very purpose and has given us the Spirit as a deposit, guaranteeing what is to come.
>
> 2 Corinthians 5:5, NIV

What is the deposit God gave us?

_____

Why did God give us this deposit?

_____

_____

What is to come?

_____

God gave us the Holy Spirit as a promise of eternal life with Christ. It's simple. When you receive the Holy Spirit, you are guaranteed entry into heaven. There is nothing you can do to break the promise of God. Only God can break His promise which is *not* in his character. Never in scripture has God broken a promise and He is not going to start now! God promised Abraham in Genesis 17:16 that he would have a son by Sarah who was unable to have children. In Genesis 21:22, Sarah gave birth to Isaac. God had a shepherd boy named David anointed king in 1 Samuel 16. Many years passed and David went from being a boy to a man before he actually became king in 2 Samuel 2. These are just two examples out of hundreds of God keeping His promises. If God kept his word to Abraham and David, He will keep His word to you!

And you also were included in Christ when you heard the word of truth, the gospel of your salvation. Having believed, you were marked in him with a seal, the promised Holy Spirit, who is a deposit guaranteeing our inheritance until the redemption of those who are God's possession—to the praise of his glory.

Ephesians 1:13–14, NIV

What happens after believing in Jesus as Lord and Savior?

_____

_____

_____

Who is the Holy Spirit?

_____

_____

Who are God's possessions?

_____

If you have accepted Jesus Christ as your Lord and Savior, you were marked with a seal of ownership by God. This seal is the Holy Spirit that guarantees your inheritance of eternal life with Christ. Only the people who are sealed with the Holy Spirit are God's possessions. If you have accepted Christ, you are God's precious possession and He loves you very much; so much that he gave his one and only son as a sacrifice for you.

> For God so loved the world that he gave his one and only Son that whoever believes in him shall not perish but have eternal life.

> John 3:16, NIV

Notice that God did not say that whoever believes in Christ and keeps a bunch of rules will have eternal life. Christ is enough! There is nothing else that can be done for salvation!

I think a lot of people confuse salvation with sanctification. There is a huge difference. Salvation is the total deliverance from sin through Jesus Christ. All that is required for salvation is faith. Sanctification is the process of becoming like Christ through the indwelling of the Holy Spirit and our dependence on Him. This includes our works and deeds. The closer we come to Christ, the more we want to do for Him. Our deeds are a byproduct of our salvation not the reason for our salvation. Without salvation, there cannot be any sanctification. We cannot become like Jesus if we do not know Him first!

> Now it is God who makes both us and you stand firm in Christ. He anointed us, set his seal of own-

ership on us, and put his Spirit in our hearts as a deposit, guaranteeing what is to come.

2 Corinthians 1:21–22, NIV

Yet again God tells us that He gave us the Holy Spirit as a deposit guaranteeing eternal life! If you find yourself struggling with this truth, ask yourself this question, "How many times does God have to say it before I believe it?" Over and over again God assures you that if you have received the Holy Spirit, you are guaranteed heaven and God never breaks his promises!

Precious one, I hope God has really touched your heart today and shown you that you are his and nothing you can do can cause you not to be his. If you have children, you can understand that. I know my children can disappoint me but there is nothing they can do that will cause me to stop loving them or disown them. It's the same way with our heavenly Father. His grace is astounding and I cannot even begin to understand its greatness. Just trust God's Word.

What has God said to you today?

_____

_____

_____

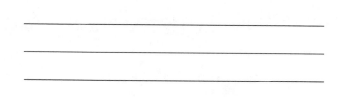

Thank God for his wonderful guarantee and reflect on his goodness today.

DAY 5

God's Property

Are you God's property? The fact is, if you do not know Jesus Christ, you are not God's property and you are a slave to sin. Everyone is a slave to something–people just don't realize it. Who or what are you a slave to? What consumes your life?

> Jesus replied, "I tell you the truth, everyone who sins is a slave to sin. Now a slave has no permanent place in the family, but a son belongs to it forever. So if the Son sets you free, you will be free indeed."
>
> John 8:34–36, NIV

Write what Jesus said in your own words.

_____

_____

_____

_____

_____

_____

Who is the Son?

_____

Jesus assures us that if we come to him, he will set us free! Does that mean that we never sin again? No. It means that the pleasure we think we get from sin goes away and loses its appeal to us. Once sin loses its appeal, we can be victorious through Christ! Amen!

> The Son of Man must be delivered into the hands
> of sinful men, be crucified and on the third day be
> raised again.
>
> Luke 24:7, NIV

> He was delivered over to death for our sins and was
> raised to life for our justification.

Romans 4:25, NIV

Why did Jesus have to die?

_____

What happened when Jesus was resurrected?

_____

Notice that Jesus was "delivered" over to death because we have sinned. Jesus never sinned. Because God loves us so much, Jesus died in our place. He paid a debt that we cannot pay. I love the word delivered because it showed that Jesus's whole reason for coming to this world was to free us from sin. In order for something to be delivered, it has to be sent—just like a letter. Almighty God humbled himself and became man just to sacrifice himself for you. The delivery was completed.

As we learned on day 3 and 4 of this week, when we accept Christ as Lord and Savior, the Holy Spirit dwells in us. In other words, God is living in us. That means that since Jesus paid our debt and now lives in us, we are to honor him. That is part of being God's property.

Do you not know that your body is a temple of the Holy Spirit, who is in you, whom you have received from God? You are not your own; you were bought at a price. Therefore honor God with your body.

1 Corinthians 6:19–20, NIV

What is your body?

_____

Where is the Holy Spirit?

_____

What is the price you were purchased?

_____

Since your body is the temple of the Holy Spirit, you should honor it as you would honor God. Do you want God to live in a shack or a temple? One of the most important things you can do is take care of yourself so your temple is radiant. Your price was so high that Christ had to give his blood as payment so keep your temple looking well.

I often have women ask me about tattoos and body piercing. They want to know if they are OK to get after becoming a Christian. My response is this: Would you like it if someone came to your church and spray painted a picture on it or put holes in the building? Most women get offended at the thought but your body is a temple of God. Anything that can corrupt your body or harm your body should not be done. You are valuable to God!

The world/society thinks it is OK to do anything, especially to your body. Just because society says that something is OK doesn't make it OK. Throughout the Bible, we are told not to live as the world does because as Christians, we are to be separate (sanctified) from the world. (John 1:10, John 15:18–19, John 17:13–17, Ephesians 6:12, 1 John 2:15–16) If you take the advise of Romans 12:2, *"Do not conform any longer to the pattern of this world, but be transformed by the renewing of your mind. Then you will be able to test and approve what God's will is—his good, pleasing and perfect will."* you will not even have the desire to do things the way the world does them. A strong statement about doing things the world's way is made in James 4:4, *"You adulterous people, don't you know that friendship with the world is hatred toward God? Anyone who chooses to be a friend of the world becomes an enemy of God."*(NIV) James was not known for beating around a bush!

Precious one if you got a tattoo or body piercing after getting saved, it does not affect your salvation–you are still God's chosen child. Also if you had things done to you before you got saved, it does not matter because you are now a new creation. The point I want to make is for you to be in God's Word. Take time each day to pray and seek God's face through His Word. If you do that, a godly life will occur naturally because God will change your heart.

> For he who was a slave when he was called by the Lord is the Lord's freedman; similarly, he who was a free man when he was called is Christ's slave. You were bought at a price; do not become slaves of men.

> 1 Corinthians 7:22–23

Before Christ, we are all slaves to sin. After Christ, we are free! How great is that?! Jesus Christ purchased you with his blood and set you free from the consequence of sin – the consequence being hell. Not only did his blood free you from hell, his blood freed you from the power of sin in your life. No matter what the sin, Christ paid for it. There is no sin that was not washed away by his blood. The blood of Christ is powerful and real.

There is an old hymn called *Nothing but the Blood* that really touches my heart because it talks about the blood of Jesus. Just mediate on the words and the truth it states or if you know the tune just sing it to the Lord. The words to the first stanza are below:

What can wash away my sin? Nothing but the blood of Jesus;

What can make me whole again? Nothing but the blood of Jesus;

Oh precious is the flow

That makes me white as snow

No other fount I know

Nothing but the blood of Jesus.

What has God said to you today?

_____

_____

_____

_____

_____

_____

_____

WEEK 2

SALVATION IS NOT . . .

This week we will look at the false doctrines concerning salvation. We are such a selfish people that we want God's plan of salvation to fit our plans and not God's. I have seen so many people that want a religion of convenience. In other words, they want God to change for them and not change for God. Salvation is all about change! We are to become like Christ and live for him. Our dependence is on Christ and nothing else. Let's see what salvation is not.

DAY 1

Salvation is Not Being Religious

I cannot go a day without hearing that Christianity is a religion and that is not true. Christianity is a relationship with Jesus Christ. A lot of people miss this point. Today's lesson will address being religious verses having a relationship with Jesus Christ. Begin today by reading Matthew 23.

To whom is Jesus talking?

_____

Who is Jesus talking about?

_____

According to verse 5, what is the motive of the teachers and Pharisees?

_____

_____

What will happen to those who exalt themselves?

_____

_____

What will happen to those that humble themselves?

_____

_____

List in your own words the seven things Jesus did not approve of with the teachers and Pharisees.

1. _____

2. _____

3. _____

4. _____

5. _____

6. _____

7. _____

In verse 33, what does Jesus call the teachers and Pharisees?

_____

_____

Write verse 39 in your own words.

_____

_____

_____

Jesus was addressing his disciples and the crowd in Jerusalem about the teachers of the law and the Pharisees. As you can tell, Jesus was not impressed with the teachers and Pharisees. Why is it so significant that Jesus was not impressed with them? They were the religious leaders of their day just like today's religious leaders: pastors, priest, Bible theologians, and ministry leaders. The Pharisees and teachers were the elite in Israel! They thought that they were better than everyone else because they followed their religion so closely. Everyone else had to come up to their standard! That is why Jesus told them that *"whoever exalts himself will be humbled, and whoever humbles himself will be exalted."* (Matthew 23:12, NIV).

There were seven issues Jesus had with the teachers and Pharisees. First of all, their talk did not match their walk. The experts could not live by the same set of rules that they set and if anyone really tried to have a true relationship with God, they stopped them. Second, the teachers and Pharisees traveled long distances to get converts to Judaism and once the people converted, they gave them impossible rules to follow. Third, they saw material things as more valuable than godly things. Fourth, they were so consumed by following the letter of the law, they forgot the real meaning or spirit of the law. Fifth, they were consumed with their outside appearance and did not take care of their hearts. Their hearts were cold and uncaring while they gave the appearance of being put together. Sixth, they saw themselves as truly righteous even though their motives were not godly. Finally, the teachers and Pharisees thought they were better than their forefathers and that they would have never committed the same sins their forefathers did–yeah right! No wonder Christ called them snakes and a brood of vipers, they were truly evil.

The teachers and Pharisees were raised Jewish and knew more about the law than the common person. What they said went! So many times I see people take firm positions on God and His Word based on what one person tells them. People form opinions and beliefs based on ignorance because they have never discovered the truth for themselves in God's Word. That is a dangerous place to be and you can be easily misled. You never take anyone's word for it; you read it yourself and ask God to give you understanding. Don't misunderstand what I am saying. I'm not saying not to listen to other people or seek advice; I am saying that you do not blindly take what anyone says as fact based on their title. This is how false doctrine gets in to the church and the only way to get rid of false doctrine is to know God's truth.

God does not want you to be religious; he wants an intimate relationship with you. If you have ever been in love—

do you remember the anticipation and excitement you had when you were waiting for the love of your life to call you on the phone? If you are like me you would sit by it, as if that would make it ring. Then when the call came you could feel butterflies in your stomach. God is waiting to hear from you with excitement and anticipation. He desperately wants you to talk to him because you are the love of His life. God doesn't need a relationship with you, God *wants* a relationship with you! My pastor, E. Truman Herring said it perfectly, "God doesn't need you to complete Him. You need God to become complete." As we close today's lesson, take time just to sit and talk with God. Tell him what is on your heart–he already knows–just tell him. Then just sit and listen.

What has God said to you today?

_____

_____

_____

_____

_____

DAY 2

Salvation is Not Based on Status

No matter what your social position, God wants you. Everyone is equal in his sight. All God wants is our hearts. Let's begin today by reading Matthew 19:16–30.

Who came up to Jesus?

_____

What did he ask Jesus?

_____

_____

List the commandments Jesus told the man to obey.

_____

_____

_____

_____

_____

_____

What did the man say about the commandments?

_____

_____

What did Jesus tell the man to do in verse 23?

_____

_____

What was the man's response?

_____

When the young man comes to Jesus, I find his question very interesting, "*Teacher, what good thing must I do to get eternal life?*" (Matthew 19:16, NIV). Notice he said "good thing"–singular. He wanted to do one thing to receive salvation but it wasn't accepting Christ which IS the one and only thing we can do to receive salvation. Possibly, his motive was an act of charity since he was wealthy and most likely had a high standing in the community. In other words, all he wanted to do was appear to do a righteous act and no commitment was involved–maybe donate some money to a near by synagogue. When Jesus told the young man to follow the commandments, he left a few out. Was that on purpose? I believe it was. The first four commandments that had to do with God were left out: no idols, do not worship idols, do not misuse the Lord's name, and keep the Sabbath day holy (Exodus 20:1–17). Even though the young man felt as if he had obeyed the 6 commandments Jesus said, he obviously did not obey the ones concerning God. This was proven when Jesus told the young man to give up everything and give it to the poor and follow him. That was more than the young man wanted. Jesus knew his heart belonged to his possessions and not to God.

If God gave salvation based on status, I am sure the rich young man would have been first in line as he certainly had status, money, and power. God does not care what position we hold! All God wants is our hearts dedicated to him. That is where the rich young man failed!

> Do not store up for yourselves treasures on earth, where moth and rust destroy, and where thieves break in and steal. But store up for yourselves treasures in heaven, where moth and rust do not destroy, and where thieves do not break in and steal.
>
> Matthew 6:19–20, NIV

Lots of people make contributions of money and time to charities and perform good deeds. These acts of kindness do not secure their salvation–salvation cannot be earned through good deeds. There is only one way to have salvation and that is to believe that you are a hopeless sinner, Jesus is

God, he died on the cross for you, was resurrected on the third day, and sits at the right hand of the Father. No status is involved! Salvation is given to us out of God's grace–grace meaning that we don't deserve salvation and we don't. God gives us eternal life out of His love for us when we come to Him through Christ.

> In him [Jesus] we have redemption through his blood, the forgiveness of sins, in accordance with the riches of God's grace that he lavished on us with all wisdom and understanding.
>
> Ephesians 1:7–8, NIV

> This righteousness from God comes through faith in Jesus Christ to all who believe. There is no difference, for all have sinned and fall short of the glory of God, and are justified freely by his grace through the redemption that came by Christ Jesus.
>
> Romans 3:22–24, NIV

Just think of the way Jesus came to this earth. He was not born of privilege in a palace with all kinds of servants. He was born in a stable that reeked with the stench of manure, his earthly father was a carpenter–not a king, his mother was a young girl with a strong faith–not a queen, and the only bed he had was an animal's trough. Certainly if the creator of the universe humbled himself to be a child of such humble beginnings, why do we think he cares what our standing is in society? Salvation is available to *all* not just the privileged!

It is not bad to be wealthy or have social status as long as your heart belongs to Christ and not your possessions. Money is not evil. Only when it takes you away from God is it evil. It depends on where your heart is and what has your devotion.

> No one can serve two masters. Either he will hate the one and love the other, or he will be devoted to the one and despise the other. You cannot serve both God and Money.

> Matthew 6:24, NIV

God knows your heart. Just like Jesus knew the heart of the rich young man. All God wants is you—just you, just as you are. He is not waiting for you to clean up your act before you come to Him. Trust Him and let Him cleanse you from the inside out. Close today by thanking God for seeing your heart and knowing the person you really are. Write Him a love letter that is between you and Him.

_____

_____

_____

_____

DAY 3

Salvation is Not a Set of Rules

Salvation is not earned by following a bunch of rules. What are some of the rules people follow? Most of the rules are based on the Ten Commandments. God doesn't sit in heaven with a check list of rules that he checks off and once you have enough checks you go to heaven. Jesus went out of his way to show that God wants your heart and not empty gestures. Let's start today's lesson by reading Luke 6: 1–11.

What day was it?

_____

Why is the day important?

_____

What did the disciples do that offended the Pharisees?

_____

_____

_____

What did Jesus say to the Pharisees?

_____

_____

_____

In verse 7, what were the Pharisees trying to do?

_____

_____

_____

What did Jesus ask The Pharisees and teachers in verse 9?

_____

_____

What did Jesus do that angered the Pharisees and teachers?

_____

_____

_____

Jesus and his disciples were walking through the grain fields on the Sabbath. What is the Sabbath? It was meant to be a day of rest where no work was done. God wants his people to take care of themselves; therefore, He commanded his people to take a day off.

Remember the Sabbath day by keeping it holy. Six days you shall labor and do all your work, but the seventh day is a Sabbath to the LORD your God. On it you shall not do any work, neither you, nor your son or daughter, nor your manservant or maidservant, nor your animals, nor the alien within your gates. For in six days the LORD made the heavens and the earth, the sea, and all that is in them, but he rested on the seventh day. Therefore the LORD blessed the Sabbath day and made it holy.

Exodus 20:8–11, NIV

As the disciples were walking, they were picking grain and eating it. This made the Pharisees angry because they looked at the commandment and not the meaning of the commandment. One of God's intentions for the commandment was for his people to rest and take care of their bodies. The disciples were taking care of their bodies! While they were literally following God, they got hungry so they ate as they walked. This gives a whole new meaning to fast food! The disciples were being obedient to the commandment but all the Pharisees wanted to do was impose their twist on God's Word.

I love Jesus's response to the Pharisees in verse 3, *"Haven't you ever read in the Scriptures what King David did when he and his companions were hungry?"* (NLT) Only God had the authority to ask such a question! That's like telling your pastor that he doesn't know what he is talking about. Those four words, "Haven't you ever read" are very powerful because Jesus is showing them that they do not understand the very scripture that they had read. Jesus reminds them that King David ate the Bread of Presence that was only for the priest to eat in the temple. The priest did not rebuke David, he gave him the bread! (1 Samuel 21:6) Who do you think understood God's command, the priest that fed David or the Pharisees that wanted the disciples to starve? In both cases, God's people were hungry and needed food for strength.

On another Sabbath, Jesus healed a man with a shriveled hand. Didn't he know the commandment? Of course he did–He wrote the commandment. Why would Jesus helping someone make the Pharisees and teachers so mad? I believe the Pharisees and teachers wanted to appear holy by following a set of rules. In their minds, they were better than the common man and here is this carpenter who doesn't follow their rules. Notice I said "their" rules and not God's rules. However, Jesus knew their evil thoughts and called them on it. He wanted to know what they found acceptable on the Sabbath: to do good or evil, to save life or destroy it. Notice not one of the Pharisees or teachers even answered Jesus and Jesus chose to heal the man. He knew it is better to help a man in need than to ignore him because someone may be offended. Because he healed the man, the Pharisees and teachers who were suppose to be the godly people, plotted against Jesus.

> Woe to those who call evil good and good evil, who
> put darkness for light and light for darkness, who put
> bitter for sweet and sweet for bitter.

Isaiah 5:20, NIV

Usually when people focus on others it's because they don't want to see themselves. It was easier for the teachers and Pharisees to try and trip up Jesus (which never happened) than to work on their walk. People can look like a Christian. People can even act like a Christian and never know God. These are truly miserable people. There are also Christians who have lost their zeal for God and feel if they just follow the rules they will be OK. It is never OK to lose your zeal for God. That means you have given up on an intimate relationship with Him! Both being a nominal Christian and being a carnal Christian yield the same results–absolute misery. It takes an intimate relationship with Christ before you can begin to understand His love.

> If I give all I possess to the poor and surrender my body
> to the flames, but have not love, I gain nothing.

1Corinthians 13:3, NIV

> And without faith it is impossible to please God, because anyone who comes to him must believe that he exists and that he rewards those who earnestly seek him.

Hebrews 11:6, NIV

No matter what you do, the only way to please God is through Jesus Christ. Only through knowing him can we follow the rules in obedience—just like the disciples did when they ate the grain. They followed the intent of the rule and that can only be done when Christ is in charge of our life. Without Christ there is no way to be able to follow God's rules because God's rules are based on a kind of love that only comes from Christ.

Are you just following the rules? Have you lost your zeal for Jesus? Take time right now to talk to God and share everything on your heart. He already knows so be honest and share it with him. God wants you to be completely happy and full of love–the only way to accomplish that is with a true relationship.

What has God said to you today?

_____

_____

_____

_____

_____

_____

DAY 4

Salvation is Not Favoritism

It is a common belief that certain sins are worse than others and cannot be forgiven. That is simply not true! Sin is sin. The only unforgivable sin is to deny Christ. It doesn't matter if someone is a serial killer, salvation is available to all. Jesus died for *all* sins not some sins. Let's start today by reading Matthew 20:1–16.

What was the agreed wage for a days work?

_____

What other times did the landowner go out and get other workers?

_____

_____

_____

What upset the workers?

_____

_____

_____

_____

What was the landowner's response?

_____

_____

_____

_____

_____

_____

Jesus is telling a parable about a landowner and the men he hires to do the work. At the beginning of the day, the landowner agreed to pay the workers a denarius which was a silver coin that was worth a day's wage–not a lot of money. The workers agreed. Throughout the day, the landowner continued to enlist help: 3 hours later, 6 hours later, 9 hours later, 11 hours later. Notice the workers that were hired first did not complain when the landowner brought more help. I am sure that they were grateful to have more help because it made their work easier. However, when it came time to be paid, the workers were angry when the workers that came at the 11th hour got paid the same as them. They thought that since they worked longer and harder they should get more. The landowner gave them exactly what he promised and told them that they would not tell him how to spend his money.

It is the same way with salvation. God is the landowner who is looking for laborers and the blood of Christ was the payment. When Jesus died on the cross, he died for *all* sin. Jesus never said that he would die for gossipers and not murders. When you examine the results of a gossiper, it is the same as a murder because a gossiper destroys people's reputations! Let's face it, destroying a person's reputation is the same in God's eyes as murdering that person because all God sees is the sin. Salvation is the most wonderful thing because no matter who you are or what you have done, it's yours—all you have to do is ask for it! What an awesome God!

> Then Peter began to speak: "I now realize how true it is that God does not show favoritism but accepts men from every nation who fear him and do what is right."

> Acts 10:34–35, NIV

The workers are us. It doesn't matter if you have been a Christian for fifty years or five minutes, the gift of eternal life is the same. Longevity does not equal greater status! If someone has been a Christian for years, they love to see new believers come to Christ. It is a time to rejoice. However, pride gets a hold of some people and they want recognition for what they have done for the Lord. If what a person does is truly for the Lord, recognition does not matter. I have seen ladies who have been saved for years get upset when a newer believer gets position or recognition in the church and that is wrong. All believers have the same salvation and the same status in Christ. God just uses people differently—that doesn't mean that one is more important than the other!

> So from now on we regard no one from a worldly point of view. Though we once regarded Christ in this way, we do so no longer. Therefore, if anyone is in Christ, he is a new creation; the old has gone, the

new has come! All this is from God, who reconciled us to himself through Christ and gave us the ministry of reconciliation: that God was reconciling the world to himself in Christ, not counting men's sins against them. And he has committed to us the message of reconciliation. We are therefore Christ's ambassadors, as though God were making his appeal through us. We implore you on Christ's behalf: Be reconciled to God. God made him who had no sin to be sin for us, so that in him we might become the righteousness of God.

2 Corinthians 5:16–21, NIV

The world has a hard time dealing with the concept of being a new creation. The moment a person is saved, they are a new creation. It doesn't matter if a person was raised in church or not, in Christ that person is a new creation. Just because a person is raised in a church does not mean that they know Christ—they can be just as lost as anyone else. No matter what a person did before knowing Christ, it is not to be held against them. The world says that people can't change but God says otherwise.

I can do everything through him who gives me strength.

Philippians 4:13, NIV

No, in all these things we are more than conquerors through him who loved us.

Romans 8:37, NIV

No matter what is in your past, with Christ it can be overcome. Salvation is the same for all who come to Christ. God does not have favorites—he loves all his children! Sometimes you may feel as if the world is against you but know one thing for sure: if you love Jesus with all your heart, soul, and strength, God is *never* against you. If you have Jesus, you have everything.

What has God said to you today?

_____

_____

_____

_____

_____

_____

DAY 5

Salvation is Not Taken Away

One of the biggest lies about salvation is that it can be lost. As we learned in day four of week one, salvation is an eternal guarantee. Today we will look at scripture that is often taken out of context and show how it is taken out of context. I feel in this instance, we need to see different translations because this will help you better understand the scripture.

> "Not everyone who says to me, 'Lord, Lord,' will enter the kingdom of heaven, but only he who does the will of my Father who is in heaven. Many will say to me on that day, 'Lord, Lord, did we not prophesy in your name, and in your name drive out demons and perform many miracles?' Then I will tell them plainly, 'I never knew you. Away from me, you evildoers!'
>
> Matthew 7:21–23, NIV

> "Not all people who sound religious are really godly. They may refer to me as 'Lord,' but they still won't enter the Kingdom of Heaven. The decisive issue is whether they obey my Father in heaven. On judgment day many will tell me, 'Lord, Lord, we prophesied in your name and cast out demons in your name

and performed many miracles in your name.' But I will reply, 'I never knew you. Go away; the things you did were unauthorized'

"Knowing the correct password—saying "Master, Master,' for instance—isn't going to get you anywhere with me. What is required is serious obedience— doing what my Father wills. I can see it now—at the Final Judgment thousands strutting up to me and saying, "Master, we preached the Message, we bashed the demons, our God-sponsored projects had everyone talking.' And do you know what I am going to say? "You missed the boat. All you did was use me to make yourselves important. You don't impress me one bit. You're out of here.'

I love the Message translation! It explains things so well. First of all, there is a huge difference between head knowledge and heart knowledge. Just because a person can quote scripture and appear godly does not mean that they have ever accepted Christ as Savior. It does not mean that they have come to the point that they realize that they are separated from God because of their sin and need the Savior. Sometimes the hardest people to reach for Christ are people that were raised in church because since birth they have been taught about Christ and encouraged to memorize scripture. Because of this, there is a false security. There has to be a point in time that where you realized you are a sinner and need Christ to save you from eternal damnation! Just because Jesus is in your mind does not mean he is in your heart.

Without Christ in your heart, it is impossible to enter heaven. I know people who have said a "salvation prayer" only to discover later that they were not saved because their heart was not ready. There is no magic prayer that can save you! Only agreeing with God about your sinful condition and asking Jesus to change your heart and be Lord of your life can save you. With salvation comes the desire for Christ and all He has to offer.

God knows the heart of everyone—there is no fooling Him. If you watch people who profess to be believers, you can usually tell who they are by their life. Unfortunately, there are a lot of people who use God to profit themselves and could not care less about people coming to Christ or knowing Him. All you have to do is turn on the television and you see every kind of charlatan who is out to get your money. Some even have the nerve to say that if you send them money, you will have salvation. God is *not* a gangster who gives salvation to those that pay him off. God already paid the price with Jesus's blood! Always ask yourself this question, "How is God being glorified through this person's actions?" What do I mean by glorified? What I mean is who is getting the attention and praise? If you do not see God being lifted up and getting the attention, chances are that person is out for themselves and not God.

True repentance causes change. If you are really sorry about something, you will do all you can to change it. That is one way you can see if your heart is right. As you grow in Christ you want to be more like Him. You never want to hurt Him and you want to do what he says. There is a difference in "playing" church and having a real relationship with Jesus.

> It is impossible for those who have once been enlightened, who have tasted the heavenly gift, who have shared in the Holy Spirit, who have tasted the goodness of the word of God and the powers of the coming age, if they fall away, to be brought back to repentance, because to their loss they are crucifying the Son of God all over again and subjecting him to public disgrace.
>
> Hebrews 6:4–6, NIV

For it is impossible to restore to repentance those who were once enlightened—those who have experienced the good things of heaven and shared in the Holy Spirit, who have tasted the goodness of the word of God and the power of the age to come— and who then turn away from God. It is impossible to bring such people to repentance again because they are nailing the Son of God to the cross again by rejecting him, holding him up to public shame.

Hebrews 6:4–6, NLT

Once people have seen the light, gotten a taste of heaven and been part of the work of the Holy Spirit, once they've personally experienced the sheer goodness of God's Word and the powers breaking in on us—if then they turn their backs on it, washing their hands of the whole thing, well, they can't start over as if nothing happened. That's impossible. Why, they've re-crucified Jesus! They've repudiated him in public!

Hebrews 6:4–6, The Message

This is a hard scripture to accept and you should pay close attention to it because there is a warning. Basically this scripture is referring to those that play church. These are the people that claim to be saved because of a head knowledge–there has never been a heart change and they come to church for a season in their life. Then someone says something that hurts them or something happens within the church and they leave and stop going to church altogether. Once that happens, their hearts become hardened to God and His Word and they have contempt for God. At this point, they have slammed the door to salvation.

Notice in Hebrews 6:4–6 there is not one mention of receiving the Holy Spirit which happens the moment a person receives Christ. It is easy to share in the Holy Spirit. Anytime the Holy Spirit works in my life, those around me saved and unsaved share in the goodness. Therefore, the people being described were never saved so they have not lost their salvation–they never had it. The sad thing is they will not receive it because they have rejected God.

Too many people think that the church should be perfect and it never will be because people are involved. Just because people go to church does not mean they have eternal life. It is dangerous to assume that everyone you encounter at church is saved. I have seen people stop serving because of someone else. I have seen people leave churches because their feelings got hurt. Let me tell you that people in church will hurt you but your walk does not depend on them so don't let it. You are held accountable for what you do or don't do and they are accountable for themselves. Others are never an excuse for your walk to suffer–especially when you are saved. I have learned from my own walk that when people offend me, I have the problem because I am looking at me and not Christ. When your focus is on Christ, you do not get offended by others comments because you give them the benefit of the doubt that their words came out wrong. Usually, that is the case. Remember, Jesus loves the saved and unsaved and so should we.

Do you attend church regularly?

_____

Do you like the church you go to?

_____

Are there people that get under you skin?

_____

If so, pray for them right now and ask God to give you a genuine love for them.

I hope after today's lesson you know for sure that salvation cannot be lost. God loves you too much to let you go. Nothing in this world can pluck you out of His hand once you are His. Only when a person is saved do they become God's child instead of God's creation. Which are you: God's child or God's creation?

What has God said to you today?

_____

_____

_____

_____

_____

_____

WEEK 3

WHERE DO THE JEWS
FIT IN GOD'S PLAN?

This week we will look at the role the Jews have in salvation. The Jews are God's chosen people; however, that does not mean that they will receive eternal life. God had a definite purpose for His people. This week we will see two major reasons why the Jews are the chosen people: 1) they were chosen through Abraham to be the people in which Christ the messiah would come 2) to bring God's wonderful Word to mankind. This will be a fun and exciting week so get ready.

DAY 1

The Law

I love God's law and hopefully by the end of today's lesson you will too—if you don't already. Sometimes the Law is a reference to the laws defined in the first five books of the Bible or Torah: Genesis, Exodus, Leviticus, Numbers, and Deuteronomy. These are known as the books of the law. There are hundreds of laws defined but they all boil down to ten. Let's begin today by reading Exodus 20.

List the Ten Commandments in order.

1. _____

2. _____

3. _____

4. _____

5. _____

6. _____

7. _____

8. _____

9. _____

10. _____

What do the first four commandments have in common?

_____

_____

_____

What do the last six commandments have in common?

_____

_____

_____

If you do not already know the Ten Commandments by heart, I urge you to memorize them. They are the foundation of our relationship to God and the foundation that America was founded on. Needless to say, they are at the core of the Christian walk.

Notice that the first four commandments have to do with our worship of God: no idols, don't worship idols, don't curse God's name, and keep the Sabbath holy. The last six have to do with our relationship to others. The order is very important because God comes first, everyone else comes second, and we are not mentioned. I know society says to look out for number 1 meaning yourself but when you are a Christian, number one is God.

> "Teacher, which is the greatest commandment in the Law?" Jesus replied: " 'Love the Lord your God with all your heart and with all your soul and with all your mind.' This is the first and greatest commandment. And the second is like it: 'Love your neighbor as yourself.' All the Law and the Prophets hang on these two commandments."

> Matthew 22:36–40, NIV

What did Jesus say is the greatest commandment?

_____

_____

_____

What did Jesus say was the second greatest commandment?

_____

_____

_____

When Jesus defined the two greatest commandments, all he did was sum up the Ten Commandments. Jesus did not repeat what the people already knew, he gave them the meaning of the law! Jesus even said that the Law of the Prophets hung on those two commandments. Wow!

I hear a lot of Christians say that Christians are not bound by the law because Jesus gave us a new covenant. It is true that our salvation is not based on the law; however, we are to live by the law. That is the only way the world will see that we are different. Jesus even clarified this point.

> "Do not think that I have come to abolish the Law or the Prophets; I have not come to abolish them but to fulfill them. I tell you the truth, until heaven and earth disappear, not the smallest letter, not the least stroke of a pen, will by any means disappear from the Law until everything is accomplished.
>
> Matthew 5:17–18, NIV

Jesus came to fulfill the law so that the Jews would see him fulfill the law and know he was the messiah. No man can fulfill the law unless the man was God—Jesus is God! Just by fulfilling the law, He proved his deity. The law is to point people to their need of salvation.

> Therefore no one will be declared righteous in his sight by observing the law; rather, through the law we become conscious of sin.
>
> Romans 3:20, NIV

For no one can ever be made right in God's sight by doing what his law commands. For the more we know God's law, the clearer it becomes that we aren't obeying it.

Romans 3:10, NLT

Before this faith came, we were held prisoners by the law, locked up until faith should be revealed. So the law was put in charge to lead us to Christ that we might be justified by faith. Now that faith has come, we are no longer under the supervision of the law.

Galatians 3:23–25, NIV

The whole purpose of the law was to show us we needed the savior. The law was never meant to impart salvation, it was meant to point to Jesus. Righteousness before God only comes through having total faith in Jesus Christ. Jesus is the only way!

I do not set aside the grace of God, for if righteousness could be gained through the law, Christ died for nothing!

Galatians 2:21, NIV

What has God said to you today?

_____

_____

_____

_____

_____

_____

Take a moment and thank God for His wonderful law.

DAY 2

Jesus in the Old Testament

You may have heard people say that there is more about Jesus in the Old Testament than in the New Testament and thought they were crazy but they were right. In most books in the Old Testament, Jesus is mentioned—not by the name Jesus but by description and/or reference. We will see a clear example of this by beginning today in Psalm 110. Please read Psalm 110 very carefully.

Who wrote Psalm 110?

_____

Write the first sentence.

_____

_____

_____

What is being described in verses 2 & 3?

_____

_____

_____

What is being described in verses 5 & 6?

_____

_____

_____

For such a short psalm, it is one of the most powerful! King David wrote this psalm. In most translations of this scripture the word LORD is used twice but they look different: LORD and Lord. There is a reason for this difference. The Hebrew word for LORD in all capitol letters is *Jehovah*3 and refers to God the Father and the Hebrew word for Lord with one capitol letter and the rest lower case is ʿ*adown*4 and refers to the Messiah or God the Son. When David says, "*The* LORD *says to my* Lord," (NIV) he is clearly speaking to the Father about his savior. Notice David said "my" Lord not "the" Lord. This shows that David knew Christ hundreds of years before Christ was even born!

David's salvation was based on the same promise we are saved by today. God promised a messiah would come and David had faith in the Messiah–the promised one. When you trust in Jesus, you have faith in the promised one. The only difference is David had faith in the promise before it was fulfilled; where as, we have faith in the fulfilled promise. God is good!

Notice how David sees Jesus. He doesn't see Jesus as a baby but as the great judge. He sees the great and final battle where God defeats Satan. People don't like to see Jesus as judge but he is. Jesus will return to judge all people and nations on earth and David saw that! David saw part of the same thing that John saw hundreds of years before John wrote Revelation! Wow! God is good!

Now read Isaiah 6:1–3, 8 and Revelation 4:2, 8.

What do these verses have in common?

_____

_____

What happens in Isaiah 6:8?

_____

_____

Both the prophet Isaiah and the disciple John saw Jesus on the throne in heaven surrounded by creatures praising him. I find it interesting that Isaiah recognized Jesus as Lord where John (who knew Jesus personally) referred to someone sitting on the throne. Maybe John did not recognize Jesus because his heavenly body looked nothing like his earthly body. I don't know the reason but I see how precious Isaiah's walk with God had to be for him to know the Lord. Jesus even spoke to Isaiah in Isaiah 6:8. Wow! I know I have said wow a lot but I am still amazed by God in all he does so forgive me for all the wows.

You may wonder how Jesus could speak to Isaiah at least seven hundred years before Christ was born. The answer is simple. Christ has always existed even before he came to earth. How do I know this? There is reference to Christ in Genesis.

> Then God said, "Let us make man in our image, in our likeness, and let them rule over the fish of the sea and the birds of the air, over the livestock, over all the earth, and over all the creatures that move along the ground." So God created man in his own image, in the image of God he created him; male and female he created them.

> Genesis 1:26–27, NIV

Notice that God said he wanted to make man in "our" image. Why would God say that? God is referring to the trinity: Father, Son, and Holy Spirit—different responsibilities but the same God. Also notice how God went from using "our" to "his" in verse 27. Why would he do that? God is referring to creating man to look like him. The only way man has ever seen God in the flesh is Jesus. So when God made reference to "his own image," he was making a reference to Jesus because Jesus is God.

Now read Daniel 9:4–10.

How does Daniel describe the Lord?

_____

_____

_____

What is Daniel Seeking from God?

_____

_____

Like David, Daniel used two references to God: LORD which is the same Hebrew word *Jehovah* that David used and Lord in which the Hebrew word is *'adoney5* and it is an emphatic meaning of the word *'adown* that David used. Also *'adoney* is the same Hebrew word that Isaiah used when he saw Jesus on the throne in heaven. I believe this shows that Daniel knew Christ and he wanted to differentiate between God the Father and God the Son just like David did in Psalm 110. Daniel's prayer is so open and touching. I do not think that it is a coincidence that when Daniel is describing the Lord (whom I believe is the Messiah) he uses words like righteous, merciful, and forgiver. These are the very qualities of Jesus. Only through a relationship with Christ can someone know his characteristics. Notice when Daniel uses LORD, he is referring to his sin against God the Father. That is no accident. When we sin it is against God the Father and reconciliation to the Father can only come through Christ the Son.

> Once you were alienated from God and were enemies in your minds because of your evil behavior. But now he has reconciled you by Christ's physical body through death to present you holy in his sight, without blemish and free from accusation—if you continue in your faith, established and firm, not moved from the hope held out in the gospel.

> Colossians 1:21–23a, NIV

Notice that Daniel was seeking forgiveness from God. He repented and asked for forgiveness. I believe this prayer is the best example of a salvation prayer from the Old Testament. To see the wisdom Daniel had is very humbling. It is easy to profess Christ after he has come but not before like Daniel did.

There are so many wonderful examples of Christ in the Old Testament and I have chosen a few to share with you. It would take a study itself to show all the references to Christ. I hope you have enjoyed today as much as I have. I get so excited every time I dive in to the Old Testament! I hope you get excited as well.

What has God said to you today?

_____

_____

_____

_____

_____

DAY 3

The Chosen People

The Jews are the chosen people. What does that mean? All it means is that God chose them to be the lineage of the Messiah and Jesus was a Jew. It does not mean that because someone is Jewish they have eternal life because birth right has nothing to do with salvation. I was born in North Carolina which is part of the "Bible Belt" but that doesn't mean I was born having eternal life. All people have to do is come to the realization that they are separated from God because of their sin. Until you realize that they are a sinner, you cannot receive salvation because you do not feel as if you need it. With that said, let's begin today's lesson by reading Matthew 22:1–14.

What is this parable about?

_____

What happens in verse 3?

_____

_____

_____

What happened in verse 5?

_____

_____

_____

What happened to the kings servants in verse 6?

_____

_____

_____

How did the king react?

_____

_____

_____

What happens in verse 10?

_____

_____

_____

What happened to the man not wearing wedding clothes?

_____

_____

_____

This parable is about a king who wants to throw a wedding banquet for his son so he sends his servants out to invite the guests. The invited guests refused to come. Again the king sent his servants out to re-invite the guests and even told them about the good food that was there so that would make them want to come but they refused. Some of them even mistreated and killed the king's servants so the king destroyed the murders and burned the city. Since the invited guests refused to come, the king ordered his servants to get anybody that would come to the banquet. When the king came and saw the guests, there was one that did not belong so he had that guest thrown out.

This parable being told by Jesus is a powerful parable because he is referencing the Jewish people and the Gentiles. The king represents God the Father and his son is Jesus, the wedding banquet is heaven, the servants are the prophets and disciples, the invited guests are the Jews, the people from the streets are the Gentiles, and the man who didn't belong is a religious person who doesn't know God. Now that all the characters are defined the story takes on a more powerful meaning.

God the Father wanted his people, the Jews, to know his son Jesus. He sent prophets to tell them about the Messiah but they refused to listen. Even after Christ was crucified, God sent the disciples out to tell his chosen people about his son Jesus. Again, the Jews rejected Jesus and some even beat and murdered the disciples. Actually, any Christian was subject to being beaten and/or murdered. Because God's own people rejected his son, he made salvation available to the Gentiles. The Gentiles accepted God's invitation and received salvation; however, there are some who are nominal Christians and God knows that. The nominal Christians are not allowed in heaven because they do not know the Son; therefore, they are cast out into hell. No one can hide their heart from God.

> Moreover, the Father judges no one, but has entrusted
> all judgment to the Son, that all may honor the Son
> just as they honor the Father. He who does not honor
> the Son does not honor the Father, who sent him.

John 5:22–23, NIV

> No one who denies the Son has the Father; whoever
> acknowledges the Son has the Father also.

1 John 2:23, NIV

There is no way to have a relationship with God without Jesus. Jesus himself tells us that he is the judge over all mankind and if you deny him, you deny God the Father. Any religion that denies Jesus is God is a false religion! The only way to heaven is Jesus Christ.

I know some messianic Jews that before they accepted Christ were scared because they thought that they would no longer be Jewish. Actually, the truth is when a Jew accepts Christ, they are still a Jew. You cannot lose your heritage but you can lose your soul. A friend of mine who is a Messianic Jew told me that before he prayed to received Christ he was scared and did not think he could do it. A friend who was with him said, "Just because a mouse lives in a cookie jar doesn't make him a cookie." At that point, my friend saw his point and he prayed to accept Christ. The mouse represents the Jewish heritage and the cookie jar represents the Gentile church. Just because the Jewish mouse now worships with Gentiles the mouse does not turn into a Gentile. No one can remove a birth right. I was born and raised in NC before I moved to Florida. Moving to Florida did not make me a Floridian. I am by birth right a North Carolinian that lives in Florida.

> Do not be afraid of those who kill the body but cannot kill the soul. Rather, be afraid of the One who can destroy both soul and body in hell.
>
> Matthew 10:28, NIV

Some messianic Jews have even been disowned by their families as traitors. Why would loving Jesus cause such a thing to happen? What about the teaching of Christ is so offensive? All Christ ever taught was love for God and each other. The fact is the world rejected Jesus and when you accept Christ, the world rejects you too.

> If the world hates you, keep in mind that it hated me first. If you belonged to the world, it would love you as its own. As it is, you do not belong to the world, but I have chosen you out of the world. That is why the world hates you.
>
> John 15:18–19, NIV

It is very important to remember that Jesus Christ was a Jew. All the disciples were Jews. The majority of Christians in the early history of the church were Jews. There is no way that a person can lose their Jewish identity by becoming a Christian! If it wasn't for the Jews, there would have been no Messiah. Without the Messiah, there would be no salvation!

> I am not ashamed of the gospel, because it is the power of God for the salvation of everyone who believes: first for the Jew, then for the Gentile.
>
> Romans 1:16, NIV

The Savior came through the Jews and we need to always remember that. No one can love Jesus and hate Jews. If anyone claims to be a Christian but they hate anyone other than Satan, they are not a Christian. Jesus loved everyone and when we accept Christ, we are to love everyone. We are to love even those people who treat us badly. That is when Christ shines the most!

What has God said to you today?

_____

_____

_____

_____

_____

_____

Take a moment and sing praises to mighty God!

DAY 4

Missing the Point

It breaks my heart to see how people miss the simplicity of Christ. I have spoken about salvation to people that tell me it is too simple and that there has to be more. There is no more than believing in Jesus and placing your faith in him! Today we are going to see how even good intentions can cause you to miss the point. Let's read Acts 7:54–8:1.

What did Stephen see?

_____

_____

_____

What was happening to Stephen?

_____

_____

_____

Whose feet were the witnesses clothes laid at?

_____

Stephen was hand picked by the apostles to work in ministry because he was known for his strong faith. It is because of his strong faith and the mighty way God was using him that the Jews convinced the elders and teachers of the law to have him arrested. When Stephen was brought before the Sanhedrin, he let them have it with both barrels. Not only did he give them a history lesson of their faith, he blamed them for Jesus's crucifixion! Needless to say, they were a little ticked off.

Stephen saw heaven open up with Jesus standing at the right hand of God. It was as if Jesus was waiting to hug his neck and letting him know that he was about to go home.

Sure enough, the people overtook him, dragged him out of the city, and stoned him to death. Saul who later became Paul was there and he watched the people's clothes while they stoned Stephen. Not only that but he approved of what was happening to Stephen.

Now read Acts 9:1–31.

Why did Saul go to the high priest?

_____

_____

_____

What happened on his way to Damascus?

_____

_____

_____

Did the men traveling with Saul see the same thing he did?

_____

What happened to Saul after seeing what he saw?

_____

_____

_____

What did God say to Ananias?

_____

_____

_____

What was Ananias's initial response?

_____

_____

_____

What was Ananias's second response?

_____

_____

_____

What happened to Saul after Ananias visited him?

_____

_____

_____

_____

Saul was part of the Sanhedrin which means he held a high position and had much power in the Jewish community. He was a Jew of the Jews and he hated Christians who back then called themselves the Way. As he saw it, the Way was destroying his religion so he wanted to destroy them. I have no doubt that Saul had a real heart for God—he just was blinded by religion and did not understand a personal relationship.

Saul had gotten permission from the high priest and was on his way to Damascus to look for members of the Way so he could arrest them and bring them back to Jerusalem as his prisoners. On his way to Damascus, he saw a bright light and heard Jesus say, "*Saul, Saul, why do you persecute me?*" (Acts 9:4, NIV). Notice Saul's response in verse 5. He referred to Jesus as Lord before Jesus told him it was him. I find it interesting that the men traveling with Saul heard a sound but never saw Jesus or the light. That just goes to show how Jesus speaks to the individual and reveals himself in different ways to people. Each relationship with Christ is different!

After Saul saw Jesus, he went blind for three days—the men with Saul had to lead him by the hand to Damascus because he was blind. Meanwhile, Saul had nothing to eat or drink for those three days.

There was a disciple of Christ named Ananias in Damascus. Jesus went to him in a vision and told him where to find Saul praying so he could lay hands on him and restore his sight. At first Ananias did not want to because Saul had a bad reputation of harming believers. After Jesus assured him that Saul was his "chosen instrument," Ananias agreed to let God use him in order to restore Saul's sight. Sure enough he found Saul and called him brother as he laid hands on Saul. Immediately, God healed him and the scales fell from Saul's eyes and his sight was restored! God is so good!

Saul's conversion on the road to Damascus is one of the most told stories in the Bible because it is one of the most significant! Not only does it show the awesome power of God, it shows how forgiving God really is to us. When Stephen was being stoned, Saul was there giving his approval. He was also on his way to arrest as many Christians as he could when he met Jesus. The Christians feared Saul and saw him as an enemy but God saw his heart. Most people would look at Saul and say that there was no hope for him. I am sure the Christians back then never saw Saul becoming one of them. God knew Saul's heart and Saul thought he was pleasing God by his actions. His faith was misguided because he depended on his religion and not on God. When he met the true God face to face, his heart was immediately changed. Not only did

God forgive him for his actions towards the Christians, he gave him an assignment! Saul obeyed Jesus. By obeying Jesus's command, he proved that his heart had changed.

> If you love me, you will obey what I command.
>
> John 14:15, NIV

The story of Saul shows how easy it is to miss the point. The point is that there is no religion that can save you. The only thing that can save you from eternity in hell is a personal relationship with Jesus Christ! No matter how good of a person you are, without Christ you have gained nothing. A lot of Christians fall in to the trap of works to replace the relationship with Christ. For example, I have seen people serving in the church that do not regularly read their Bibles or have time with God each day. They think that serving God earns them brownie points. The truth is if you are not in the Word daily and spending some quiet time with God, you have no business serving. How can you serve a God that you do not know personally? That would be like trying to buy clothes for a person you don't know well and have to guess at their size. If you spend time with God daily, you don't have to guess at his size—you know it.

It is also easy to miss the point when you put faith in traditions and not in Christ. There are so many beautiful rituals within the church (different by denomination) that are meant to point to Christ but because people do not know the meaning of the ritual, they put their faith in the ritual. Take for example baptism–it symbolizes the death, burial, and resurrection of Christ. When a person is baptized, they are publicly saying that Christ is in charge of their life. Baptism has nothing to do with salvation! If you accept Christ as Lord and die before you get baptized, you will not go to hell! Baptism is the first step of obedience a new believer takes in their walk with Christ. There is no magical power in the water–it's just water.

No matter how good your intentions are, if you leave Christ out, you have missed the point. Christ should be in *every* area of your life. After Saul's conversion he became Paul the great apostle. Every aspect of his life revolved around Christ. Paul even wrote most of the New Testament while in prison for his faith. He went from being the persecutor to being the persecuted! Jesus is everyday not just on Sundays.

How has your walk been? Have you put your faith in everything else except Christ? Are you a Christian that struggles with a relationship with Christ? Take a moment and write a personal letter to God–it can be as long or short as you want. Tell him everything on your heart–he already knows but you need to let it go. The space is provided for you.

DAY 5

Return to God

Today we will see why salvation was given to the Gentiles and how much God wants his chosen people to come back to Him. God will not force someone to love Him—that's why he gave us freewill. He is waiting with open arms for his beloved to return to him. Today we see Israel through the eyes of Paul. Let's begin by reading Romans 11:1–24.

Has God rejected the Jews?

_____

How did Paul describe himself?

_____

_____

_____

According to verse 5, what is there?

_____

_____

_____

Why did salvation come to the Gentiles?

_____

_____

What was Paul's hope?

_____

_____

Who are the broken off branches?

_____

Who is the wild olive shoot?

_____

Who is the root?

_____

Why were the branches broken off?

_____

_____

What will happen to the broken branches if they stop their unbelief?

_____

_____

God did not reject the Jews! The apostle Paul described himself as an Israelite, a descendant of Abraham, from the tribe of Benjamin so that people would see that God had not rejected him and he was a Jew. Throughout the Old Testament when God would punish Israel in all kinds of ways, including death, he always left a remnant because of his promise to Abraham. Paul explains in verse 5 that there is a remnant chosen by grace. What does that mean? It means that there are Jews that believe in Jesus and they are the remnant—all the others have turned away from God. Paul explains this in verse 7, "*What then? What Israel sought so earnestly it did not obtain, but the elect did. The others were hardened,*" (Romans 11:7, NIV). The elect are the believers in Christ and they are the only ones that have a true relationship with God. Israel as a whole does not have a relationship with God, only the elect do. That may be a little hard to swallow but God's Word does not lie.

Salvation came to the Gentiles because Israel rejected the true God. God wants the Jews to be jealous of our relationship with God so they will seek to have the same kind of relationship. That was also Paul's heart. He wanted his ministry to be so great to the Gentiles that his own people would get jealous and want to know God through Christ. Paul wanted his precious people to be saved. He knew birth right or tradition had nothing to do with salvation. If that were the case, Paul would not have needed it himself because he was the Jew of the Jews. Also if tradition or birth right had anything to do with salvation, there would be no hope for anyone except the Jews. God's gift of salvation is so precious that he offers it to *all* through Christ. All people have the opportunity to receive salvation!

> That if you confess with your mouth, "Jesus is Lord," and believe in your heart that God raised him from the dead, you will be saved. For it is with your heart that you believe and are justified, and it is with your mouth that you confess and are saved. As the Scripture says, "Anyone who trusts in him will never be put to shame." For there is no difference between Jew and Gentile—the same Lord is Lord of all and richly blesses all who call on him, for, "Everyone who calls on the name of the Lord will be saved."
>
> Romans 10:9–13, NIV

Paul used the illustration of an olive tree to explain his point about salvation: the broken off branches are the Jews that have rejected God, the wild olive shoot is everyone who is not Jewish–Gentiles, the olive root is Jesus, and the olive tree is God the Father. When the Jews decided to worship other gods and turn their back on God the Father, their branches were broken off which means that they do not fellowship with God. If someone rejects God, they cannot have an intimate relationship with Him. The Gentiles who were not originally part of God's people were grafted into the olive tree by believing in Jesus Christ. Only through Christ are the Gentiles allowed to fellowship with God. Since Jesus is the olive root, He maintains the health of the tree–he keeps the fellowship with all those that profess him as Lord. Jesus sustains his followers, they do not sustain him! In Christ, there is no room for arrogance among believers because all believers are branches. Some branches may be a little stronger than others, some may have knots all in it, and some may be struggling to grow but they are all part of the same tree and they should all work together. Different branches have different uses–that doesn't mean one is more important than the other.

> Then Peter began to speak: "I now realize how true it is that God does not show favoritism but accepts men from every nation who fear him and do what is right."

> Acts 10:34–35, NIV

For God does not show favoritism. Romans 2:11, NIV

Notice that there is always hope in God. Paul explains that even if a branch has been broken off, it can be grafted back into the olive tree. If a Jew that has been raised in tradition and never put their faith in Christ changes and believes in Christ, that Jew will have fellowship with God through Jesus. In other words, they will be restored. God never gives up on His people. God is so good!

My desire is that you realize how precious the Jewish people are and that just because they were born Jewish does not mean they have eternal life. Salvation is a choice that everyone must make. You either choose Christ or you don't. There is no sitting on the fence. If you want to sit on the fence, you have chosen not to accept Christ. Salvation is an all or none kind of a thing. There is no room for compromise. Look at what Jesus says.

> He who is not with me is against me, and he who does not gather with me scatters. And so I tell you, every sin and blasphemy will be forgiven men, but the blasphemy against the Spirit will not be forgiven.
>
> Matthew 12:30–31, NIV

Where do you stand with God today?

_____

_____

_____

_____

_____

_____

What has God said to you today?

_____

_____

_____

_____

_____

_____

WEEK 4

Proof of Salvation

There is no way to know what is in a person's heart–only God knows that; therefore, it is impossible for me to tell you beyond a shadow of a doubt who has eternal life. There are Christians who live defeated lives because they do not depend on Christ, they depend on themselves. That doesn't mean that they have not accepted Christ, it just means that Jesus is not Lord of *their* life on a daily basis. There is a big difference between Jesus as Savior and as Lord. This week we will look at evidence that will help you determine if someone is really a Christian. Like I said, there is no way to know a persons heart; however, *"the things that come out of the mouth come from the heart."* (Matthew 15:18a). Remember, actions always speak louder than words.

Core Beliefs

What is a core belief? A core belief is something you will not compromise on and will even put your life on the line if necessary. A core belief is not based on a lie because people do not willingly give their life for a lie! Today we will look at two apostles, Peter and John and see what their core belief was. Let's read Acts 4:1–31.

Who put Peter and John in jail?

_____

_____

Why were Peter and John put in jail?

_____

_____

_____

Who questioned Peter and John?

_____

_____

Who did Peter give credit for healing the cripple man?

_____

_____

Who is Peter talking about in verse 12?

_____

Write verse 12.

_____

_____

_____

What were Peter and John told not to do?

_____

_____

What were Peter and John's response?

_____

_____

_____

Peter and John were on their way to the temple to pray when they came a cross a crippled beggar who asked them for money. *"Then Peter said, 'Silver or gold I do not have, but what*

I have I give you. In the name of Jesus Christ of Nazareth, walk.'"
(Acts 3:6, NIV) After Peter helped the beggar up, he started
praising God. The commotion caused people to come over
to Peter and John to see what was happening. Peter used this
to God's advantage by sharing the gospel to everyone around
him. This greatly upset the temple priest, the captain of the
temple guard, and the Sadducees so they had Peter and John
arrested and put in jail for talking about Jesus.

There were a lot of people that came to see Peter and
John questioned: the rulers, elders, and teachers of the law. All
the people that questioned Peter and John are mentioned by
name: Annas the high priest, Caiaphas, John, Alexander, and
other men from Annas's family. Annas was the father-in-law of
Caiaphas (John 18:13) who was the high priest when Jesus was
crucified. Both men were responsible for the death of Jesus so
they definitely did not like what Peter was saying. The people
questioning Peter and John did not want to hear the truth
because they had their minds set on what they wanted. Knowing this, Peter told them the beggar was healed by the name of
Jesus Christ and reminded them that they were the ones who
crucified him. Talk about making a bad position worse!

Not only did Peter quote scripture to them, he told
everyone that could hear him his core belief in verse 12. Peter
was willing to die for his core belief! He knew the truth

and he wanted everyone else to know the truth. It was Peter and John's courage that made the high priest and his family sit back and take notice. What could cause two uneducated men have such courage and knowledge? Only God!

Since the healed beggar was standing with Peter and John, the miracle could not be denied so Peter and John had to be set free. However, they feared the spreading of the gospel so before letting Peter and John go, they commanded them not to teach or speak in the name of Jesus. I love the way Peter responded with another one of his core beliefs in Acts 4:19–20, *"Judge for yourselves whether it is right in God's sight to obey you rather than God. For we cannot help speaking about what we have seen and heard."* Peter was more concerned about obeying God than man.

> Then the eleven disciples went to Galilee, to the mountain where Jesus had told them to go. When they saw him, they worshiped him; but some doubted. Then Jesus came to them and said, "All authority in heaven and on earth has been given to me. Therefore go and make disciples of all nations, baptizing them in the name of the Father and of the Son and of the Holy Spirit, and teaching them to obey everything I have commanded you. And surely I am with you always, to the very end of the age."
>
> Matthew 28:16–20, NIV

Jesus commanded Peter to spread the gospel and to make disciples so Peter was willing to die and remain obedient to Christ rather than live and please man. Only a true knowledge of Christ and the truth can cause such a passion for obedience!

Immediately after being released from jail, Peter and John went with other believers to pray. I love the way Peter prayed for boldness. If he wasn't bold before the high priest and his family, I don't know what he was! I am sure Peter was scared and that is why he prayed for boldness. By his actions, he showed another core belief—all things are possible with God. When Peter surrounded himself with other believers to pray and sought God for strength, God answered in a powerful way and gave everyone praying boldness. Wow! God is good!

What are your core beliefs?

_____

_____

_____

Are your core beliefs the same as Peter's?

_____

_____

If you claim to be a Christian, you should believe the following:

Jesus is God

Jesus died for your sins

Jesus was resurrected on the third day

Jesus sits at the right hand of God the Father

These beliefs cannot be compromised in any way. This should be the core belief of your faith. If it is not, there is no way that you can have a personal relationship with Christ. If it is what you believe but you feel hopeless, chances are you are living under condemnation–you do not feel worthy to be around other Christians because of things you are doing or have done. Jesus meets us where we are at not where we want to be. If you are living under condemnation, talk with God right now and tell him everything on your heart then surround yourself with Christian friends by regularly attending a Bible preaching church, and read God's Word daily. This way you will destroy the depression and hopelessness that come from condemnation and replace it with the joy of your salvation!

What has God said to you today?

_____

_____

_____

_____

_____

What is your response to him?

_____

_____

_____

_____

_____

DAY 2

Obedience

The word obey is mentioned in God's Word over 200 times. Obedience to God is very serious and the way we prove to others that we love God! Today we will look at a story where obedience was necessary to live. Let's read Numbers 21:4–9.

What was the people's attitude toward God?

_____

_____

_____

What did God do?

_____

_____

_____

What was the people's attitude when they went to Moses?

_____

_____

_____

What did God tell Moses to do?

_____

_____

_____

What did the people have to do in order to live after being bitten?

_____

_____

_____

The Israelites were stuck in the desert because they did not have enough faith to go into the Promised Land—they were scared. So for 40 years they wondered around and God provided them manna from heaven. Needless to say, they were sick and tired of manna! Instead of being grateful to God for having their needs met, they wanted more and were ungrateful.

Not only were the Israelites ungrateful, they began to speak badly of God and constantly complain. God sent venomous snakes to their camp and many people died from snake bites. Ouch! When this happened, the people went running to Moses (as always) and asked him to pray for them.

Their attitudes went from ungrateful to repentant. Moses did pray for them and God told him to make a pole and put a snake on it. Anyone who got bitten could look up at the pole and live. So Moses built a pole and put a bronze snake on it.

Why would God have Moses put a bronze snake on a pole? Why would doing this cause people to be healed? It is simply a matter of obedience! People could choose whether or not to look up at the snake. If any one thought, "It is stupid to look up a pole at a bronze snake! I am not going to look up."—they died. It was simple, look at the snake on the pole and live or don't look and die.

This story is a foreshadowing of Christ. The venomous snakes represent sin and we have all been bitten. No one is sinless except Jesus! The bronze snake and pole represents the curse of sin and judgment which caused Jesus to die on the cross. When Moses nailed the bronze snake to the pole, he was showing that God's judgment was complete and all they needed to do to be saved was believe Him and obey. When Jesus died on the cross, he took the judgment for our sin—death. Also, it showed that the cross defeated sin. Anyone who believes in Christ and obeys him is saved. Notice when the Israelites went to Moses, they were repenting of their sin against God. So before they looked up at the bronze snake, they had to be sorry for their sin. It is the same way before a person can come to Christ. You first have to realize that you are a sinner and are sorry for your sins. Only through repentance can obedience happen!

> Just as Moses lifted up the snake in the desert, so the Son of Man must be lifted up, that everyone who believes in him may have eternal life.
>
> John 3:14–15, NIV

> Jesus replied, "If anyone loves me, he will obey my teaching. My Father will love him, and we will come to him and make our home with him. He who does not love me will not obey my teaching. These words you hear are not my own; they belong to the Father who sent me."
>
> John 14:23–24, NIV

> This is how we know that we love the children of God: by loving God and carrying out his commands. This is love for God: to obey his commands. And his commands are not burdensome, for everyone born of God overcomes the world. This is the victory that has overcome the world, even our faith.
>
> 1 John 5:2–4, NIV

The only way to prove that you do love Jesus is to obey him! If others hear you say that you are a Christian and you do not obey Christ, your actions speak much louder than your words! The only way to know what Jesus says is to read the Bible daily. If you do not know what the Bible says, how can you ever expect to obey Christ? God has given you the tool you need for obedience—use it! You can't hammer a nail with out the hammer and you cannot obey God unless you know what he says.

> The man who says, "I know him," but does not do what he commands is a liar, and the truth is not in him. But if anyone obeys his word, God's love is truly made complete in him. This is how we know we are in him: Whoever claims to live in him must walk as Jesus did.
>
> 1 John 2:4–6, NIV

If you think it is too hard to follow Christ or you have to give up too much, you have a heart problem. The only cure is Jesus. Only Jesus can change a heart and when he does, you want to do exactly what he says. There is no longer you, it is all about Him. Like I said, only through repentance can there be obedience. Obeying rules does no good when God is not at the center. Man's rules and God's rules don't always agree!

Who would you rather obey, God or man?

Who are you obeying right now?

_____

_____

What has God said to you today about your obedience
to Him?

_____

_____

_____

_____

_____

_____

DAY 3

Love for Others

I think the most misunderstood word is love. People see love as a wonderful feeling that makes them feel good. That is not real love. Real love is obedience–doing what God says for someone else even if you do not like that person. Let's see what Jesus had to say about this, read Luke 6:27–36.

What are we suppose to do to our enemies?

_____

_____

Who are you to bless?

_____

Write verse 31.

_____

_____

What will give you a great reward?

_____

_____

Now read Luke 10:25–37.

What was the question the teacher of the law asked Jesus in verse 25?

_____

_____

What was Jesus' response?

_____

Who was the first person to pass by the man beaten half to death?

_____

Who was the second to pass the man beaten half to death?

_____

What did the Samaritan man do for the man beaten half to death?

_____

_____

_____

Jesus tells us to love our enemies and do good to those that hate us. According to the world's standards, you are justified when you get even with someone that did you wrong but that is the opposite of God's standard. God's standard is based on the supernatural. The natural person hates their enemies and tries to get even; whereas a Christian depends on the supernatural power of Christ to love their enemies. Only through a relationship with Jesus Christ can you bless those that curse you and pray for those that mistreat you. Jesus said if we love our enemies, do good to them, and lend them stuff without expecting it back, our reward will be great! Wow! Jesus never promised it would be easy!

When the teacher of the law asked Jesus, "*What must I do to inherit eternal life?*" Jesus asked the teacher how he interpreted the law. When the teacher wanted clarification on whom his neighbor was, Jesus told the parable of the Good Samaritan. I love the parable of the Good Samaritan. It is the perfect example of what Jesus was talking about when it comes to loving your enemies.

A man that was traveling from Jerusalem to Jericho when he was robbed. The robbers stole all his clothes and beat him so badly that he was half dead. I am sure that by looking at him he looked dead. Keep in mind that this man was most likely a Jew. Imagine the man lying on the side of the road, scratched up, bruised, bleeding, and humiliated. He was unable to help himself and all he could do was hope that someone would help him. Imagine what the man was thinking (if he was conscience) as he saw the priest, a holy man, coming toward him . . . the excitement he felt . . . only to be disappointed when the priest passed by and because he had no strength he couldn't even call out for help. Again he may have gotten excited when he saw the Levite, another holy man, coming toward him . . . only to be crushed as he too would pass on by and not help. I am sure that the poor beaten man was wishing he could die so the humiliation would end. Then he sees the Samaritan–one of those half breeds that the Jews did not like because they were not real Jews. Imagine the man's bewilderment when the Samaritan bandaged his wounds, took him in town to an inn, paid for the inn and left him. I wonder what was going through his mind and if his opinion of Samaritans changed.

Notice the two holy men walked right on by the man. This is an example of following the law to the letter but missing the meaning. The meaning of the law was summed up accurately by the teacher of the law in Luke 10:27 *"Love the Lord your God with all your heart and with all your soul and with all your strength and with all your mind; and, Love your neighbor as yourself."* (NIV). Jesus said these laws were the greatest two commandments in Mark 12:28–31. Yet according to Jewish law, anyone who touched a dead body was to be unclean for seven days (Numbers 19:11) which means they were separated from others for seven days until they could be made ceremonially clean again. As a matter of fact, a priest was not to even be in the presence of a dead body (Leviticus 21:11). God never intended the law to be used as a way to avoid helping others in need. Neither man took the time to see if the beaten man was dead or not; therefore, they may have followed one part of the law but actually broke the law in its entirety by not helping the beaten man. It is like when we see someone in need and we do nothing because we do not want to get involved—we are just as guilty as they were.

> Anyone, then, who knows the good he ought to do
> and doesn't do it, sins.

> James 4:17, NIV

I love the way Jesus uses a Samaritan as the hero in his parable. The Jews did not like the Samaritans because they were half Gentile and half Jewish as we saw on day three of week one in this study. By Jesus using the Samaritan as the hero, he was saying that it is not important where you came from; it is your character that is important. The Samaritan had good character and followed the meaning of the law better than the priest or Levite. He understood what loving his neighbor really meant. God does not look at position, he looks at the heart! Not only did the Samaritan help him on the side of the road, he went out of his way to make sure the beaten man would be OK. That is a wonderful example of what it means to be a Christian.

The word Christian means Christ like. In other words, we are to be a reflection of Him. It is detrimental to God when someone says they are a Christian and their character doesn't match. The number one character trait for a Christian is to be concerned about others before yourself. You cannot be the center of your world and expect Christ to be glorified or in control. There can only be one driver and God does not force you out—you have to give control to God. Once God has control, the love for others is a supernatural byproduct that comes from a dependence on God.

How do you think others would describe you?

_____

_____

_____

Do you think they see you as loving others or yourself?

_____

_____

_____

When is the last time you did something for someone else?

_____

_____

_____

_____

What has God said to you today?

_____

_____

_____

_____

_____

_____

Take time today to reach out to someone in love: write them a note, give them a call, stop in and visit, cook a surprise for them. Just do something for someone that shows them you really love them.

DAY 4

Fruit in Life

When someone is a born again Christian, there will be proof in their life or their walk with Christ. This proof is often referred to as fruit. Let's see what Jesus had to say about people's fruit in Matthew 7:15–20. Please read Matthew 7:15–20.

What did Jesus tell us to watch out for?

_____

_____

How will we recognize them?

_____

What can a good tree *not* produce?

_____

What can a bad tree *not* produce?

_____

What happens to the bad trees?

_____

_____

Jesus warns us to watch out for false prophets who say that they love Jesus and their lives prove the exact opposite. It is by the way they live their lives that we will recognize them. Always ask yourself, "Do their actions match what they say?" If the answer is no, more likely than not, they are a false prophet! Jesus tells us that a good tree cannot produce bad fruit. In other words, a true Christian cannot behave in a way that is contrary to the Holy Spirit. For example, if someone claims to be a Christian and their lifestyle is in contradiction of the Christian beliefs and they justify their sin with no remorse—chances are that person is not a Christian! A bad tree is someone with a head knowledge of Christ and never accepts him as Lord or has never believed in God. There are certain character traits that come with being a born again Christian and without Christ, it is impossible to have them.

> But the fruit of the Spirit is love, joy, peace, patience, kindness, goodness, faithfulness, gentleness and self-control. Against such things there is no law.

> Galatians 5:22–23, NIV

It is impossible for a bad tree to have all the characteristics that come from the Holy Spirit. They may have one or two but not all. Notice "fruit" is singular which means all the character traits are part of the same fruit. In contrast, the bad tree has characteristics that are opposed to the good tree.

> The acts of the sinful nature are obvious: sexual immorality, impurity and debauchery; idolatry and witchcraft; hatred, discord, jealousy, fits of rage, selfish ambition, dissensions, factions and envy; drunkenness, orgies, and the like. I warn you, as I did before, that those who live like this will not inherit the kingdom of God.
>
> Galatians 5:19–21, NIV

Since the bad tree and the good tree are exact opposites, there is no way the bad tree can give good fruit; therefore, the bad tree is burned up. What was Jesus saying when he said the bad tree would be cut down and thrown into the fire? If you have not accepted Christ and become a good tree, you are condemned to hell for eternity. I didn't say that—Jesus did and he is God. If you have an apple tree with root rot, you will not get beautiful apples. What would you do with the bad apple tree—cut it down or leave it hoping for apples? No matter how much you hope, apples will never grow on a tree with root rot. If you do not have Christ, you are the tree with root rot and the only way for you to grow apples is to come to Christ so he can restore your root. Without Christ, there can be no good fruit.

> The good man brings good things out of the good stored up in his heart, and the evil man brings evil

things out of the evil stored up in his heart. For out of the overflow of his heart his mouth speaks.

Luke 6:45, NIV

Not only does a person's character show their heart, their actions do as well. If you truly love Christ, you want to do everything you can for him. People should see you doing all you can to glorify God. I have seen women serve God for a season and stop as if their sentence is over. Serving God is not a sentence or punishment, it is a privilege and we should do it joyfully. When you serve God joyfully, people are able to see him working in your life and it encourages them. When you do not want to serve God or do it begrudgingly, you discourage others.

How do you feel about serving God?

_____

_____

_____

_____

What do you like or dislike about it?

_____

_____

_____

_____

What good is it, my brothers, if a man claims to have faith but has no deeds? Can such faith save him? Suppose a brother or sister is without clothes and daily food. If one of you says to him, "Go, I wish you well; keep warm and well fed," but does nothing about his physical needs, what good is it? In the same way, faith by itself, if it is not accompanied by action, is dead. But someone will say, "You have faith; I have deeds." Show me your faith without deeds, and I will show you my faith by what I do. You believe that there is one God. Good! Even the demons believe that—and shudder.

James 2:14–19, NIV

In order to be fruitful in your walk with Christ, you need action. A Christian is to be active in service so that God is glorified. It is impossible for people to know your love for Christ if they don't see your actions! The old cliché is right–actions do speak louder than words. People will not consider your faith relevant if what you say does not match your actions.

If you are active in service, you will never know all the lives you touch. The little things you do that you think nobody sees are actually the things that end up touching people the most. I have seen floral arrangements lift ladies spirits–that is fruit. I have seen people make meals for others who are sick and seen how an unbelieving family was impacted–that is fruit. A lot of times we do not get to know how much fruit we have but one thing is for sure, if you lovingly serve God, you have fruit!

I hope you have been encouraged by today's lesson. I hope it has helped you to be able to discern true Christians from nominal Christians.

What has God said to you today?

_____

_____

_____

_____

_____

_____

What do you want to say to God today?

_____

_____

_____

_____

_____

_____

DAY 5

Humility

I know the word humble gets thrown out a lot but what does it mean to be humble? A humble person is gentle, patient, submissive, not arrogant, and not prideful. A humble person realizes that their world is not all about them but about others. Just because a person is humble does not mean that they are a door mat or will not make a stand for something they believe in strongly. Their heart focuses other people's needs. Jesus is a perfect example of humility. Let's begin today by reading John 13:1–17.

What did Jesus do for his disciples?

_____

_____

How did Peter respond in verse 8?

_____

_____

Write what Jesus said to Peter in verse 8.

_____

_____

_____

How did Peter's response change?

_____

_____

_____

Why did Jesus do this for his disciples?

_____

_____

_____

I love this story of how Jesus washed his disciples' feet! It really shows the power and love of humility. Just think Jesus, the God man, knelt down beside a water basin and washed the feet of his disciples'. Wow! Back then there were no paved roads, just dusty streets with animal dung as decoration. There were no sneakers but sandals so all the dirt and grime from the streets adhered to their feet. I am sure their feet stunk badly from all the heat and sweat and there was no such thing as foot deodorant. Washing the disciples' feet was a disgusting job! Jesus wasn't focusing on the task but on teaching what true humility is all about.

At first Peter did not want his Lord to wash his feet but when Jesus told him that he could not have anything to do with him if he did not wash his feet, Peter's tune changed very quickly! I love the way Peter wanted to belong to Jesus so badly that he told Jesus not to stop at the feet but to do his hands and head too. What an awesome display of love on Peter's part.

Jesus's whole reason for washing his disciple's feet was not for attention or any other reason but to teach humility. He expected his disciples to do everything he did. He never wanted them to feel as if they were better than others. That's why he did one of the most disgusting jobs possible so they could see that there is no room for pride or arrogance in

God's kingdom. Pride is the very reason Satan was thrown out of heaven (Isaiah 14:12–15, Luke 10:18). Notice Jesus did not announce his intention to wash their feet–he just did it. If nothing is beneath God, nothing should be beneath you.

> The greatest among you will be your servant. For whoever exalts himself will be humbled, and whoever humbles himself will be exalted.
>
> Matthew 23:11–12, NIV

> He has brought down rulers from their thrones but has lifted up the humble.
>
> Luke 1:52, NIV

> Be completely humble and gentle; be patient, bearing with one another in love.
>
> Ephesians 4:2, NIV

> He mocks proud mockers but gives grace to the humble.
>
> Proverbs 3:34, NIV

God cannot stand pride because pride is at the root of all sin. If you claim to be a Christian, you should want God to do whatever is necessary to rid you of pride. Only through humility can we be like Christ. Jesus himself taught humility through action and if you want to follow him you must be humble. It is a daily battle that is why Jesus said in Luke 9:23, *"If anyone would come after me, he must deny himself and take up his cross daily and follow me."* (NIV). Only through Christ can humility be achieved.

I hope you have enjoyed this study of salvation and that you have had some questions answered. If you have come to the realization that you do not really have a relationship with Jesus Christ, you can change that right now. Just thank Christ for dying on the cross for you, ask God to change your heart, ask Him to forgive you for everything you have done against Him, ask Him to be Lord of your life and today will be your day of salvation. Praise God! The truth is that God sought you before you sought him and he is waiting with open arms for you right now.

If you are a born again Christian but you have lost the joy of your salvation, tell God right now exactly how you feel–he already knows so just tell him. The next step is to call a Christian friend and begin praying about where God wants to use you. Allow Him to direct you and trust Him. Let God be in control because he will not force you to give him control–you have to give control. Study your Bible daily and ask God what he wants you to learn. Only through spending time with God and serving him will you grow and get the joy of your salvation back.

Where do you stand with God right now?

_____

_____

_____

_____

Where do you want to be with God?

_____

_____

_____

_____

What has God revealed to you through this study?

_____

_____

_____

_____

Thank you for allowing me to be a part of your life for the last 4 weeks. I have truly enjoyed this time and hope you have as well. God bless you!

Endnotes

1. Bold word added by author.

2. Paragraph based on a sermon by Pastor Scott Opalsky.

3. Blue Letter Bible. "Dictionary and Word Search for *'Y@ hovah (Strong's* 03068*)'* "Blue Letter Bible. 1996–2002. 21 Jul 2006. <http://www.blueletterbible.org/cgi-bin/words.pl?word=03068&page=1>

4. Blue Letter Bible. "Dictionary and Word Search for *"adown (Strong's* 0113*)'* "Blue Letter Bible. 1996–2002. 21 Jul 2006. <http://www.blueletterbible.org/cgi-bin/words.pl?word=0113&page=1>

5. Blue Letter Bible. "Dictionary and Word Search for *"Adonay (Strong's* 0136*)'* "Blue Letter Bible. 1996–2002. 21 Jul 2006. <http://www.blueletterbible.org/cgi-bin/words.pl?word=0136&page=1>